An opini

QUEER
LONDON

Written by
Frank Gallaugher

Adonis (no. 29)

INFORMATION IS DEAD.
LONG LIVE OPINION.

London: if it's queer, it's definitely here. One of the premier cities in the world for LGBTQ+ life, with *so* much on offer it can be hard to figure where to go. This is where we come in. And this is where we'd send you if you were to come and crash on our couch for the weekend.

Here you'll find everything from infamous West End gay bars to not-so-secret underground clubs in Dalston, from film festivals and art tours showcasing queer trailblazers to raucous drag brunches. We've sorted the fierce and fresh from the tired and tame so we're confident you'll enjoy only the cream of the capital's scene.

Other opinionated guides:

This page: Clapham Grand (no. 36)
Opposite: UK Black Pride (no. 22)

Queer House Party (no. 10)

This page: Pride in London (no. 3)
Opposite: The Karaoke Hole (no. 21)

THERE'S MORE TO QUEER
LONDON THAN SOHO...

The oft-repeated statistic that 60 per cent of London's queer venues have closed in the last decade might make you think the capital's queer scene is on life support and desperately in need of new clientele. In truth, we've just been a victim of our own success – queer is cool now, so everywhere is queer. You can go to a drag brunch at an All Bar One these days, and if that's your bag, more power to you. But it's not for us. We're after that authentic, sometimes gritty, often transgressive yet always inclusive taste of queer culture that refuses to be assimilated and still proudly asserts and celebrates its differences.

This isn't just some academic study either. While there's plenty of fascinating queer history to learn along the way, we're usually just looking for a good time – and the queers can always be trusted to serve it to you. Our art lines gallery walls, our fashion defines the industry, our stories are told through riveting theatrical spectacles and – needless to say – our dancefloors are always the place to be on a Saturday night. Culture follows queers wherever we go, and the rich tapestry of our creative expression is deeply woven into this city's art institutions. We can't help but show it off! From films and festivals to cabaret and karaoke, queer folk are natural entertainers. We love to draw a crowd, so it's no wonder our events are invariably welcoming and inclusive.

All this brings with it a built-in community that's the envy of many lonely Londoners. We're lucky to have dedicated outreach groups like the LGBTQ+ Community Centre (no. 43) and Opening Doors (no. 12), but all the best queer venues (i.e. the ones in this book) nurture their community in their own way. Speak up in a discussion after a Vito Project viewing (no. 42) and people will actively seek out your opinion next time; the waiters at Balans (no. 49) know their regulars so well that some nights feel like family reunions; and the friendships among the trans community at the WayOut Club at the White Swan (no. 19) go back decades. Queer people take care of each other – it's a legacy from our more marginalised days that continues to bring wildly different people together into a chosen family.

It's these people that make each event and location worth a visit. Clapham Grand (no. 36) is a gorgeous venue and the menu at The Cockatoo (no. 18) is one of the best in town, but without the queers, who cares? The people you'll meet through this guide are some of London's most interesting, so strike up a conversation with your bartender, give your drag queen a big tip, fall in and out of love, and live your best life exploring all that this queer city has to offer.

Frank Gallaugher, 2023

SEASONAL EVENTS

Some seasonal events in the queer calendar are so monumentally massive they are deserving of their own entries (hello, Pride!), but special mention also goes to the following, which are well worth making a pilgrimage into the city for.

QUEER EAST

Ring in the spring with this vibrant festival of LGBTQ+ cinema and live arts from East and Southeast Asia. Now in its fourth year, there's a diverse programme of film premieres, shorts, music, and dance performances exploring what it means to be queer and Asian.

Spring / queereast.org.uk

DRAG FEST LONDON

This feast of fun comes to London in August and is an un-adulterated display of eyebrow-arching camp. Expect drag legends a plenty on the main stage, as well as a lip-sync stage, glitter stations, market stalls, funfair and meet-and-greets.

Summer / klubkids.co.uk/drag-fest

WORLD AIDS DAY RED RUN

Join in with the 5K or 10K runs, or just show your support and bask in the community spirit. Organised by the tireless campaigners at Positive East, this annual HIV fundraiser in east London's Victoria Park has previously featured special guests such as Sir Ian McKellen and Dame Barbara Windsor, with the race soundtracked by DJs from Horse Meat Disco and Eagle London.

Autumn / redrun.org.uk

GAYWISE FESTIVAL®

GFest is an inclusive LGBTQ+ arts festival with a jam-packed agenda of exhibitions, performances, readings, screenings, music, comedy and debates. At various venues across the capital every November (including most major galleries), the launch parties have even previously been held in the Houses of Parliament.

Autumn / gaywisefestival.org.uk

LGBTQ+ HISTORY MONTH

Every February, the capital sashays back in time with this fascinating foray into London's sometimes secret history and celebrates its queer trailblazers. Running for nearly 20 years, there's an impressive calendar of events with everything from film screenings to cultural tours and art extravaganzas.

Winter / lgbtplushistorymonth.co.uk

FRINGE! QUEER FILM AND ARTS FEST

This week-long festival has a grassroots feel and features a truly expansive roster of events across east London. Expect the usual films, panels, parties and performances, but also creative writing groups, intimacy workshops and health and wellbeing events.

Winter / fringequeerfest.com

1

GAY'S THE WORD

London's queer literary emporium

Of course, there are the books – a masterfully curated canon of queer literature that the erudite staff are happy to share their knowledge of (recommendation cards scattered throughout combine superb taste with witty summaries – 'Be trans, do crimes!' for Jordy Rosenberg's *Confessions of the Fox*). But that's just scratching the surface: for over 40 years, the notice boards, discussion groups, author talks and radical political organisations hosted here have fostered every facet of London's queer community. These days you're more likely to see a mum browsing with her trans teen than activists planning their legal defence, which proves just how successful this institution has been.

66 Marchmont Street, WC1N 1AB
Nearest station: Russell Square
gaystheword.co.uk @gaysthewordbookshop

2

LONDON GAY MEN'S CHORUS

Britain's biggest boyband

First off, if you fancy joining then put this book down and go online right now to sign up for the waiting list, because it's about 1–2 years long. This is just to give you some idea of how popular this 30-year-old institution is. At least you'll have plenty of time to prep for your audition, and lots of opportunity to see them perform, from Christmas carols at Liberty to packed houses at Cadogan Hall, Ally Pally and the Royal Albert Hall. With costumes, choreography and plenty of camp, the performances are joyously exuberant. Try to stop yourself from singing along – we dare you.

Performing at various venues across London
lgmc.org.uk @ldngmc

3

PRIDE IN LONDON

Soho at its carnivalesque best

The parade is great (even if it has become a bit of an opportunity for corporate rainbow-washing), but if you can't get a decent viewpoint, you don't have to miss out on the fun. Gather a crew together, douse yourselves in glitter, and get down to Soho – it's a queer carnival atmosphere with the streets closed to traffic, stages set up for music and cabaret, community stalls to check out (particularly around Soho Square), and a vibe that only exists for one day a year. When you get the chance to take over a whole neighbourhood in central London, you seize it!

Old Compton Street, W1D 6HH
Nearest station: Tottenham Court Road
prideinlondon.org @prideinlondon

4

HEAVEN

Approaching 50 and still divine

It's one of the first and most famous gay superclubs on the planet – and yes, that notoriety guarantees long queues and pricey drinks so get a discount wristband from G-A-Y in Soho and race over before midnight. There's still no place like Heaven. With its world-class sound system pulsating beats across two full dance floors and reliably raucous crowds every night, as long as you come here committed to dancing your face off you will have the time of your life. Lose your friends, make new ones, lose them too, then stumble out and treat yourself to breakfast at Balans (no. 49) – it's a Soho rite of passage.

9 The Arches, Villiers Street, WC2N 6NG
Nearest station: Embankment
g-a-yandheaven.co.uk @heavenlgbtclub

5

BISHOPSGATE INSTITUTE

Hidden gem of queer heritage in the City

Behind the magnificent stone turrets is an embarrassment of riches for the cultured queer. You can take a guided tour of the LGBTQ+ archives, or even a walking tour of queer Bloomsbury. Fancy a dance? There's Pink Jukebox for ballroom and Latin, and Queer Tango London speaks for itself. The calendar is packed with workshops and panels on everything from queer fanfiction to London's kink and fetish history. It's been carrying on the Victorian legacy of providing free cultural institutions to the people of London for over 125 years, and its embrace of all things LGBTQ+ is testament to the impact of queer culture on the city.

230 Bishopsgate, EC2M 4QH
Nearest station: Bishopsgate
bishopsgate.org.uk @bishopsgateinst

6

ELECTROWERKZ

Wild nights worth dressing up for

With six rooms across three floors, including a covered cobblestone courtyard, this massive warehouse accommodates London's wildest theme nights. From Torture Garden (fetish) and Riposte (queer art rave) to Roast (bears and beefcake) and House of Trash (Bimini's party), half the fun is dressing the part, and the queue for the cloak room is long enough to give plenty of time to change if you don't want to travel there in your party gear. Once suitably attired, get lost in the stripped-back, raw-brick labyrinth. Plenty of bars means service is reasonably quick (if pricey), and by the time you've made several circuits of the cavernous space, the sun will be rising.

7 Torrens Street, EC1V 1NQ
Nearest station: Angel
electrowerkz.co.uk @electrowerkz

ELECTROWERKZ
VENUE, BAR & RESTAURANT

NON - FERROUS
SCRAP METAL MERCHANTS

LEAD
£ PER CWT

BRIGHT COPPER
WIRE
£ PER CWT

NO UNAUTHORISED
PARKING

SCRAP
BRASS
WANTED

7

HAMPSTEAD HEATH PONDS

Wild swimming in an urban oasis

The Victorian prudishness that designated separate bathing ponds for men and women has, in a delicious irony, produced the gayest strip of green space in the city. When it's hot, Highgate Men's Pond is transformed into London's gay beach, where you're equally welcome to strut about in a speedo or sit back and spectate, and that's just in the free area outside the ponds, while the nearby Kenwood Ladies' Pond has its own queer community. A few years back, the City of London saw fit to start charging a fee to swim, and you'll need to book ahead in summer, but there's simply nothing else like it in London – a pastoral enclave where the camaraderie is palpable.

Hampstead Heath, NW3 1BP
Nearest stations: Gospel Oak, Kentish Town

8

QUEER BRITAIN

The UK's only dedicated LGBTQ+ museum

It's a good thing the team behind this hard-won and long overdue space is ambitious, because packing the stories of countless queer Brits into its handful of rooms is no small feat. In its mission to chronicle the roots of the rebellious communities that laid the foundations of queer British culture, the museum pulls together artefacts from across the country, including the cell door behind which Oscar Wilde was imprisoned for 'gross indecency' and a rainbow hijab worn by members of Imaan (the UK's largest LGBTQ+ Muslim charity). Witnessing them all in one place inspires a genuine sense of pride. The volunteers are eager to chat and founts of knowledge about queer venues and events in the city as well as its gay pioneers.

2 Granary Square, N1C 4BH
Nearest station: King's Cross St Pancras
queerbritain.org.uk

X
DESIGN

PRIDE

The Queer Bible — DR JACK GUINNESS
The Queer Bible — DR JACK GUINNESS
The Queer Bible — DR JACK GUINNESS
The Queer Bible — DR JACK GUINNESS
The Queer Bible — DR JACK GUINNESS

GAY BAR — WHY WE WENT OUT — JEREMY ATHERTON LIN

GAY BAR
GAY BAR
GAY BAR
GAY BAR
GAY BAR

100 QUEER POEMS

AN ANTHOLOGY BY
MARY JEAN CHAN
ANDREW McMILLAN

PRETTY CITY LONDON
PRETTY CITY LONDON
PRETTY CITY LONDON

PETER ACKROYD QUEER CITY
PETER ACKROYD QUEER CITY
PETER ACKROYD QUEER CITY
PETER ACKROYD QUEER CITY
PETER ACKROYD QUEER CITY
PETER ACKROYD QUEER CITY

HER and QUEER

PRIDE
THE STORY
OF THE
LGBTQ EQUALITY
MOVEMENT
MATTHEW TODD

GAY'S THE WORD BOOKS

Gay's The Word is the UK's oldest
LGBTQ bookshop. Founded in
1979, it also acted as a much-needed
community space. Especially for us,
they've selected the edit of books
you'll find around our shop. Visit
them in Marchmont Street, near
Russell Square tube.

9

ATLAS GRINDS

Queer neighbourhood cafe bar

The rotating influx of locals gives this low-key venue a Central Perk vibe, where excellent coffee, vegan and vegetarian snacks, and reliable wi-fi make it easy to cosy up in a corner for a few hours with a book or laptop. Stay long enough and you'll find yourself in a poetry reading, book launch, Eurovision viewing party or any number of other queer events that owner Daniel Fico regularly welcomes into this friendly, cheerful space. The secluded garden out back feels miles away from the high street, and with Giddy Hour every day from 5–7pm, there's a relaxed dynamism to this queer hub that makes it hard to pack up and leave.

155 Stoke Newington High Street, N16 0NY
Nearest station: Stoke Newington
atlasgrinds.co.uk @atlasgrinds

10

QUEER HOUSE PARTY

Accessibility, activism and anarchy

When three DJ flatmates decided to throw a Zoom party early in the first lockdown of 2020, they just wanted to show their friends a good time. Word got out, thousands started joining each online event, and QHP's unique blend of punk queerness and radical inclusivity catapulted the collective to the forefront of London's queer music scene. Now they've opened for Years & Years at Wembley, are a staple on the festival circuit, and host IRL parties in various venues across town (often to be found at the Garage in Highbury). They've made accessibility an integral part of their performances, live-streaming events and providing sign language interpreters, audio descriptions and closed captioning that ensures everyone can join the party.

Online and at venues across London
@queerhouseparty

11

THE KING'S HEAD THEATRE

Pub theatre with impeccable pedigree

Standing head and shoulders above the rest of Islington's buzzy theatre scene, The King's Head has been presenting avant-garde spectacles in its intimate space for over 50 years. It kickstarted the careers of legends Richard E. Grant and Alan Rickman, and continues to dedicate itself to performances that are 'joyful, irreverent, colourful, and queer'. The theatre is moving in autumn 2023 to a new space with double the seating capacity, a few feet to the right in Islington Square. The new venue will pay homage to the theatre's history and glittering acting alumni, but you can still grab your pre-show drinks at the original Victorian pub.

116 Upper Street, N1 1QN
Nearest station: Angel
kingsheadtheatre.com @kingsheadthtr

12

OPENING DOORS

*Community and companionship
for LGBTQ+ over-50s*

We're not all fortunate enough to have older queer friends, and far too many of our seasoned kings and queens are living in social isolation. Opening Doors bridges this gap with events across London, including meetups, art groups, IT clinics and personal connections that volunteers regularly report have changed lives. The charity is successful enough that face-to-face befriending is oversubscribed, but don't wait for the next round of recruitment – volunteers are welcome at almost all the regular events. Younger generations benefit hugely from the campaigning of those who came before, and the companionship of older queer folk helps put Peter Pan syndrome in perspective.

*Events take place across London
openingdoors.lgbt @openingdoorslgbtq*

13

BETHNAL GREEN WORKING MEN'S CLUB

Rough diamond with a heart of gold

The faded 1960s decor should help you picture the scene: back at the turn of the millennium, owner/curator Warren Dent made a pitch to the old East End members that the best chance of saving their 19th-century club was to open the doors to queens, cabaret and raucous hipster dance parties. It totally worked, and the BGWMC (save your breath) went on to incubate far more queer events than we could possibly list here. But to get started, you won't be disappointed with Pink Glove (indie/new wave disco), Pussy Liquor (patriarchy-smashing cabaret), or the Double R Club (a surreal phantasmagoria of faggotry).

42–46 Pollard Row, E2 6NB
Nearest station: Bethnal Green
workersplaytime.net @bgwmc

14

VFDALSTON

Social revolution through disco

This bastion of gritty authenticity in Dalston's nightlife scene has been a refuge for queer East End artists since fashion designer and founder Lyall Hakaraia migrated his epic three-day house parties down to his basement back in 2007. You'll doubtless miss the nondescript sign by the door, so look out for a politically charged art display in a shop window instead – that'll be The Outsiders Gallery, VFD's rotating exhibit which gives a taste of the transgressive spirit of protest that permeates all the events here. The dance parties are a hot mess (in the literal, sweaty sense), the performances are some of east London's edgiest, and there is a genuine feeling of community.

66 Stoke Newington Road, N16 7XB
Nearest station: Dalston Kingsland
vfdalston.com @vfdalston

15

DALSTON SUPERSTORE

Quintessential queer pleasure palace

There's a special alchemy here that manages to feel inclusive and achingly hip at the same time, but you'd expect nothing less from the epicentre of east London's queer scene. Along with VFD (no. 14) just down the road, Superstore fuses Dalston's art and queer scenes, with heavy emphasis on minority support for its Black, trans and lesbian communities. By day it's a cafe/restaurant/art gallery with an all-vegan menu, hosting the best drag brunch in the city every Sunday afternoon. By night there's a dedicated party for every demographic, each of which pairs pandemonium with positivity, giving you a safe space to let loose.

117 Kingsland High Street, E8 2PB
Nearest station: Dalston Kingsland
dalstonsuperstore.com @dsuperstore

16

THE GLORY

Showtime on the Haggerston Riviera

The grande dames of London drag, Jonny Woo and John Sizzle, established this hothouse of queer creativity in order to pass the torch on to the next generation of performance artists. Miles from your rehearsed Soho queens, these shows are avant-garde and unapologetically unpolished. As the premier venue for up-and-coming queer performers, it's no wonder The Glory also hosts London's biggest drag competition, LIPSYNC 1000, with eight weekly runoffs in May and June, leading up to the final at the Clapham Grand (no. 36). Whatever show you're seeing, order a cocktail and strike up a conversation with your bartender – they're all well-connected east London creatives, so when they give you a recommendation, follow it.

281 Kingsland Road, E2 8AS
Nearest station: Bethnal Green
theglory.co @thegloryldn

17

COLOUR FACTORY

Warehouse club and safe space

Just across from The Yard Theatre (no. 27) in Hackney Wick, this vibey venue hosts some of east London's biggest club nights and always provides a safe space for queers, even if it's not an explicitly queer event. But when they want to be explicit... well, there's Hard Cock Life (gay hip hop), Pxssy Palace (for queer and trans women of colour), Harpies (trans striptease), and HOWL (a big queer rave that often features all of the above), to name a few of our favourites. And just so you never have to leave, it also houses a food court – the vegan Hogless Roast is to die for.

8 Queen's Yard, E9 5EN
Nearest station: Hackney Wick
colourfactory.com @colourfactorylondon

18

THE COCKATOO AT BISTROTHEQUE

Dinner theatre with a bite

For special occasions, nothing beats the fine-dining experience at this buzzy Bethnal Green culinary institution, particularly when you add on a ticket to the Cockatoo. The modern European menu is the same (outstanding), you'll just trade the airy upstairs dining room for an intimate lounge-style space. After a boisterous dinner set to a banging soundtrack, indulge in the cocktail menu and strap yourself in, because there's no stage, the immersive performance takes place in and around the booths. The performers are invariably well-known names in queer culture, but the roster is constantly changing so it's worth planning ahead to make sure you see your favourite act.

23–27 Wadeson Street, E2 9DR
Nearest stations: Cambridge Heath, Bethnal Green
thecockatoo.london

19

THE WHITE SWAN

Wear what you want; be what you want

Because sometimes you need a break from the rest of east London's hipster-than-thou scene, we're grateful that The White Swan keeps to its working class, pretension-free roots in all its tacky neon glory. Cybil's House is your best bet: the reliably chaotic fancy-dress party that always feels fresh with a new theme every month. And as the new home of The WayOut Club, there is no place in the capital more welcoming of the trans community. It's no exaggeration to say that hostess Vicky Lee put the T in the LGBTQ+ movement, and she's spent 30 years building a safe, celebratory space that countless trans Londoners call home.

556 Commercial Road, E14 7JD
Nearest station: Limehouse DLR
bjswhiteswan.com @thewhiteswanbar

20

BODY MOVEMENTS

The UK's first queer and trans music festival

For one day every summer, the streets of Hackney Wick reveal an ecstatic vision of queer utopia when the LGBTQ+ scenes from every corner of the capital converge and explode across a dozen venues in a kaleidoscope of corsets, fishnets, glittering half-naked bodies and electronic music. Amid the gyrating dancers and hypnotic beats, a profound sense of gratitude is tangible – we're lucky to be able to partake in this full-spectrum display of queer joy and liberation. Fortunately, there's also a Winter Edition to power you through the darkest days of the year by conducting the same electricity into a massive all-day indoor rave.

Hackney Wick
Nearest station: Hackney Wick
bodymovements.co.uk @bodymovementsfestival

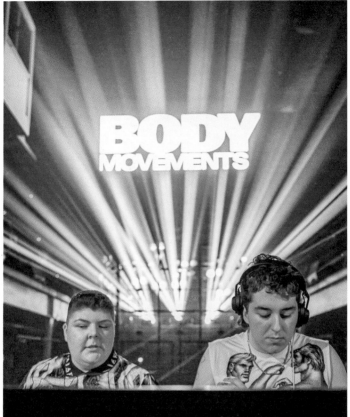

21

THE KARAOKE HOLE

Loud, proud and chaotically kitsch

The premise couldn't be simpler: pack a bunch of queers in a basement, give them cheap cocktails and free pizza, and let their inner divas take over. The whole frenzied affair is barely held together by a few indefatigable drag queens, an app that keeps the song queue in order, and a spirit of shameless stupidity that makes serenading strangers with reckless abandon feel perfectly normal. The chemistry of it all just works, no doubt borrowing a bit of Superstore's alchemy from just upstairs (no. 15). It's perfect for rowdy birthday celebrations, but with groups of any size be sure to book ahead as it fills up fast.

95 Kingsland High Street, E8 2PB
Nearest station: Dalston Kingsland
thekaraokehole.com @thekaraokehole

22

UK BLACK PRIDE

Pride with purpose

We'll say it: Pride in London (no. 3) has become a corporate-sponsored mainstream mess. Every summer, UK Black Pride offers something different; founded in 2005 by the inimitable activist Lady Phyll, it's a celebration of African, Asian, Middle Eastern, Latin American and Caribbean-heritage LGBTQ+ people, focusing on the unique experience of these vibrant but often discriminated-against communities. The festivities (incredible food, passionate performances and better dancing than you'll see anywhere in Soho) are infused with a healthy dose of community outreach and a strong sense of purpose, and while it remains an inclusive event, white queers can take a turn being supportive allies rather than the focus of attention.

Queen Elizabeth Olympic Park, E20
Nearest station: Stratford
ukblackpride.org.uk @ukblackpride

23

GUTS GALLERY

Queer art you won't find anywhere else

Guts is dedicated to disrupting London's exclusive art scene by specifically showcasing minority ethnic, queer and working-class artists, and its full calendar of 11 exhibitions a year (with regular group shows) proves that founder Ellie Pennick's inclusive approach is paying off. From Shadi Al-Atallah's representations of the queer ballroom scene and African dance traditions to Juan Arango Palacios' tracking of queer identities across migrant diasporas, the brave, intimate and challenging works on display here are an invigorating breath of fresh air amid the typical gallery gatekeeping of London's art scene. Don't miss the next opening.

Unit 2, Sidings House, 10 Andre Street, E8 2AA
Nearest station: Hackney Downs
gutsgallery.co.uk @guts_gallery

Shadi Al-Atallah, *Power Trip*, 2023

24

BARBERETTE

Don't pay extra for your gender

The hair salon can be a weirdly discriminatory space – particularly so for gender non-conforming queer folk, but also simply for short-haired women who are tired of paying more for the same cut as the bloke in the chair next to them. Klara Vanova and her team of stylists remedy this with a refreshingly straightforward approach: a set menu with prices based on hair length, an exceedingly inclusive safe space, and in-depth knowledge of the trends and styles their clientele want. With regulars hanging around for a chat, and rotating art exhibits lining the walls, it's no wonder they've built up a dedicated base of return customers.

Studio 11, Warwick Works, Lower Clapton, E5 8QJ
Nearest station: Rectory Road
barberette.co.uk/london @barberette_original

25

THE COMMON PRESS BOOKSHOP

Connecting the discriminated against

This colourful, contemporary space updates the standard gay bookshop format for the 21st century by embracing not just queer literature, but also Black and minority authors, ecocriticism, reproductive justice, disability activism and marginalised voices across every genre – plus a cafe and children's reading room thrown in for good measure. With Brick Lane just around the corner it has a bustling vibe, helped by the impressive calendar of author readings, book clubs, writing circles and even voguing workshops. That's a lot to pack in, and yet it doesn't feel cramped – in fact, it's a great date spot if you can nab one of the tables.

118 Bethnal Green Road, E2 6DG
Nearest station: Shoreditch High Street
thecommonpress.carrd.co @thecommonpress

26

GILBERT & GEORGE CENTRE

Art for all in the heart of Spitalfields

Having spent well over half a century making art together as an openly gay couple, the East End's most enduringly eccentric duo now have their own centre to show off their signature blend of provocation and traditionalism. A former brewery, it's a huge space encompassing three gallery rooms in which their colossal works fill the walls like stained glass in a cathedral. Best of all, Gilbert and George themselves can often be found standing idly around in the bookshop, ready for you to pose a question – just don't expect a straight answer.

5a Heneage Street, E1 5LJ
Nearest station: Aldgate East
gilbertandgeorgecentre.org @gilbertandgeorgecentre

27

THE YARD THEATRE

Provocative productions with parties to match

As a radical theatre, inclusive community centre and host to some of the capital's wildest queer dance parties, The Yard Theatre is plugged in to the most creative outlets in east London. You can follow a cabaret circus with a Big Queer Banquet one day, network with creatives at Queer Clash Diary the next, then get a ticket for the annual NOW theatre festival and spend the spring watching six shows for £60. There's no denying it though, most people know The Yard for its dance parties: from the joyous Knickerbocker and techno-charged Inferno to the transmasc T-Boys Club and Fast & Bi-Furious rave nights, there's a party tailored to every demographic.

Unit 2a Queen's Yard, E9 5EN
Nearest station: Hackney Wick
theyardtheatre.co.uk @theyardtheatre

28

THE QUEEN ADELAIDE

Arty boozer with a wild side

This cosy, unassuming East End pub is a favourite spot on the local art student scene, which could almost explain why there's a proper art gallery in the toilets. No, really: the White Cubicle Toilet Gallery has exhibited local and international artists since 2005 as an antidote to London's commercial art scene. The warren of rooms that make up the rest of the downstairs host an eclectic and unpredictable mix of LGBTQ+ dance nights every weekend. Don't spend too much time trying to decipher the flyers – you can't go wrong on a weekend here, so just show up and get your groove on.

483 Hackney Road, E2 9ED
Nearest stations: Cambridge Heath, Bethnal Green
thequeenadelaide.com @thequeenadelaide

29

ADONIS

Debauchery in docklands

Next time a friend starts waxing nostalgic for the bygone glory days of London's 'proper' club nights, toss them into the throbbing, carnal dance-floor of docklands' Adonis. DJ Shay Malt has managed to combine the mayhem of Berlin's club scene with London's fashion and irreverent wit, creating a monthly party that revives pre-internet underground rave culture. The sultry dark room is a hedonistic destination in its own right, where you'll witness a pulsating tableau of flesh that makes cruising clubs feel tame. While the crowd naturally skews young, it's genuinely intergenerational in scope, which adds to the unpretentious and celebratory spirit. Everyone here knows this is something new, exciting, and worth all the sweat.

60 Dock Road, E16 1YZ
Nearest station: Silvertown DLR
adonis.eventcube.io @adonis.adonis.adonis

30

MIGHTY HOOPLA

London's biggest and brightest music festival

It's not every day that you get to sing along with 25,000 costumed queers to your favourite early noughties power ballads – specifically, it's the two days in June when Brixton's Brockwell Park hosts the carnival of camp that is Mighty Hoopla. Headliners like Charli XCX and Years & Years draw crowds from afar, but local collectives such as Queer House Party (no. 10), Outhaus and Queer Bruk keep it an authentically London affair. Brace yourself for a full-throttle sensory overload of glitter, sweat and neon, and pace yourself – because you get to do it all again on Sunday.

Brockwell Park, SE24 0NG
Nearest station: Brixton
mightyhoopla.com @mightyhoopla

31

THE EAGLE

Pub with disco vibes and art show atmosphere

It's got famously friendly staff and a spacious patio out back, but really you come to The Eagle for two simple reasons: Duckie (Saturday) and Horse Meat Disco (Sunday) – two of London's most legendary club events. HMD has spent two decades perfecting its unique blend of funk and disco that is unlike any other dance floor in town: groovy, goofy and joyful. Duckie has been around even longer, and this eclectic arts collective puts on a daytime show every Saturday from 2–8pm, with £3.50 pints, £10 bottles of house wine, and a rotating roster of avant-garde queer artists.

349 Kennington Lane, SE11 5QY
Nearest station: Vauxhall
eaglelondon.com @eagleldn

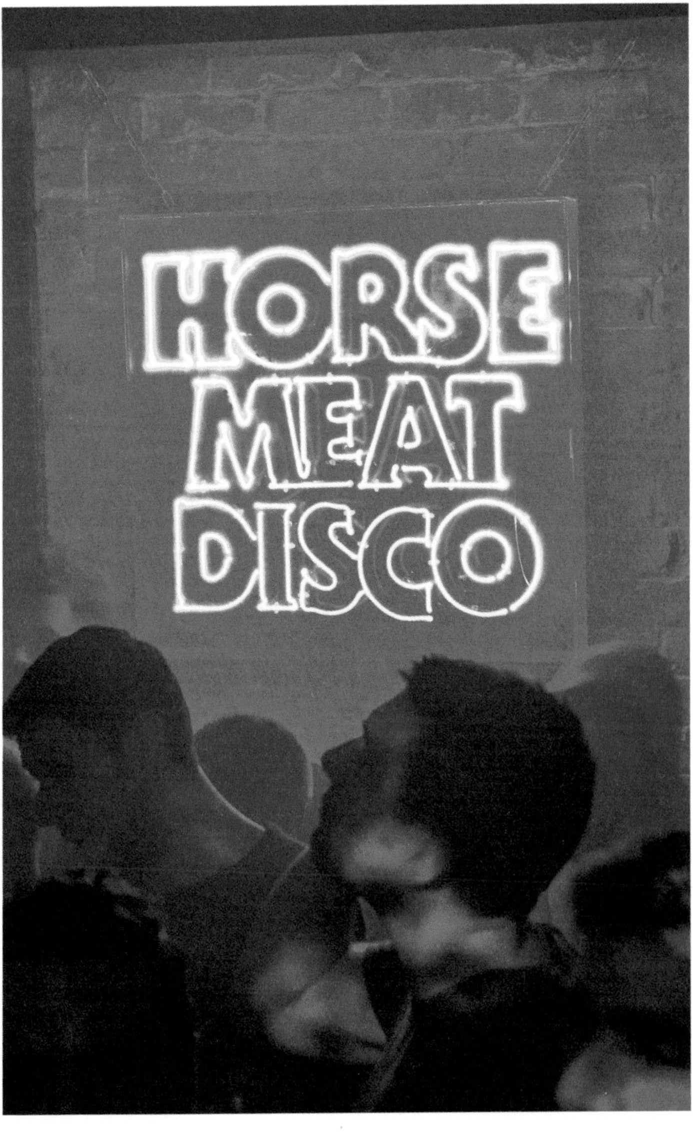
HORSE
MEAT
DISCO

32

BFI FLARE

London LGBTQIA+ Film Festival

For around two weeks every March, BFI South-bank rolls out the red carpet for LGBTQ+ stories from every corner of the globe in a cinematic celebration that makes the queer London experience feel quaint. Plan ahead and go along with your well-thumbed brochure, because between the films, galas, panel discussions and Big Gay Film Quiz, there's far more on offer than any one cinephile can consume. Part of the superpower of being queer means you are connected to people in faraway places that you'll never visit, and BFI Flare is the best opportunity to witness their loves, lives, struggles and triumphs.

0 Belvedere Road, SE1 8XT
Nearest station: Waterloo
bfi.org.uk/flare @bfiflare

33

PHILIP NORMAL

Camper than Christmas, and with better gifts

Can't think of a present for a friend of Dorothy? You literally cannot miss this Brixton Village indie shop – it's got enough neon to glow in the daylight. The eponymous artist and designer slaps his sassy slogans on everything from t-shirts to teacups to tote bags (Murder, She Tote), and also collaborates on the collection with artists across London, from up-and-comers to established names like David Shrigley. The brand is part retro pop culture, part in-your-face queer, often hilarious, with some genuinely stunning fashion and art pieces mixed in, and always worth a browse. Even if you don't buy anything, you're guaranteed a giggle!

45 Brixton Village, Coldharbour Lane, sw9 8pr
Nearest station: Brixton
philipnormal.shop @philipnormal

34

THE COCK TAVERN

Former tiki bar in a Georgian building

Eponymous jokes aside, you'll be struck by how classy the Cock feels when you first walk in, with its vermilion walls, art deco chandeliers and wide polished-wood bar. Then, feeling dozens of eyes staring at you, you'll notice the array of framed portraits carefully mounted all across the ceiling. By the time you get to the Hawaiian-themed dance floor at the back, the quirky personality of this 'Georgian tiki' tavern is readily apparent. Choose a glass from the extensive cocktail list, settle in at one of many cosy tables, and watch as this dignified establishment gradually descends into a late-night dance party.

340 Kennington Road, SE11 4LD
Nearest station: Kennington
thecocktavernlondon.com @thecocktavernlondon

35

THE VAULTS THEATRE

Immersive theatre in graffiti-lined tunnels

There's underground theatre, and then there's the subterranean spectacle carved out beneath the arches of Waterloo station. The Vaults Theatre puts on London's finest am-dram, with queer remixes of pop-culture classics like *Mulan Rouge* (a Disney/Luhrmann mashup), *Stranger Sings* (a parody musical based on the blockbuster Netflix series), and *The Witches of Oz* (Dorothy in drag). The lavish set pieces and interactive performances transform the warren of intimate spaces and envelop the audience in the atmosphere of each show. Like a camper, queerer Secret Cinema, the Vaults serves up immersive dinner theatre without taking itself too seriously.

Launcelot Street, SE1 7AD
Nearest station: Waterloo
thevaults.london/theatre @thevaultslondon

36

CLAPHAM GRAND

Palace of modern variety

The majestic red Mansfield stone facade houses an opulent 1,250-seat chinoiserie-styled theatre decked out in pagodas and dragons – and that's before the queens even get on stage. The Grand has been going strong since 1900, when it was founded by the original pantomime dame Dan Leno. These days, it's where the most famous international touring drag acts come to perform, and where local parties like BeefMince ('bear-full and attitude-free') and SlayStation (drag and video games combined) host their biggest bashes of the year. As a true variety hall, its inclusivity extends beyond the LGBTQ+ crowd, so be sure to check what's on or you might show up to an MMA fight night by accident.

21-25 St John's Hill, SW11 1TT
Nearest station: Clapham Junction
claphamgrand.com @theclaphamgrand

37

BUTCH, PLEASE!

Bringing the love, respect and power to club nights

Femmes on Top, Butch Plaid, Sporty Dyke, Hot Butch Summer – the endless themes of 'London's coolest lesbian club night' are testament to both its welcoming attitude (dyke-centred but inclusive of all lesbian and bisexual women, trans and non-binary people) and the riotous variety of London's butch scene. Making the best use of the RVT's space (no. 39), there are punk performances, skill shares, drag kings and a whole lot of making out on the dance floor. With not a cis male in sight, this is the most refreshing celebration of female masculinity anywhere in the capital.

Twice a month at the Royal Vauxhall Tavern,
372 Kennington Lane SE11 5HY
Nearest station: Vauxhall
butchplease.co.uk @butchpleaselondon

38

ARCH

Best of Clapham's gay triumvirate

It's tempting to pull a hat-trick when you see Bridge, Fetch and Arch lined up side by side beneath Clapham's overground viaduct, but of the three you'll want to linger longest in the latter. Arch opens at midday, offers an impressive menu (including Sunday roasts), and welcomes remote workers with solid wi-fi and plenty of USB ports. By all means pop down to Bridge at happy hour (two cocktails for £12 from 5–7pm) but get back to Arch in time for the entertainment: Quiz Night Tuesdays, Karaoke Wednesdays, Drag Bingo Thursdays, and DJs with go-go dancers on the weekends.

Arch 642, Voltaire Road, sw4 6DH
Nearest station: Clapham North
archclapham.co.uk @archclapham

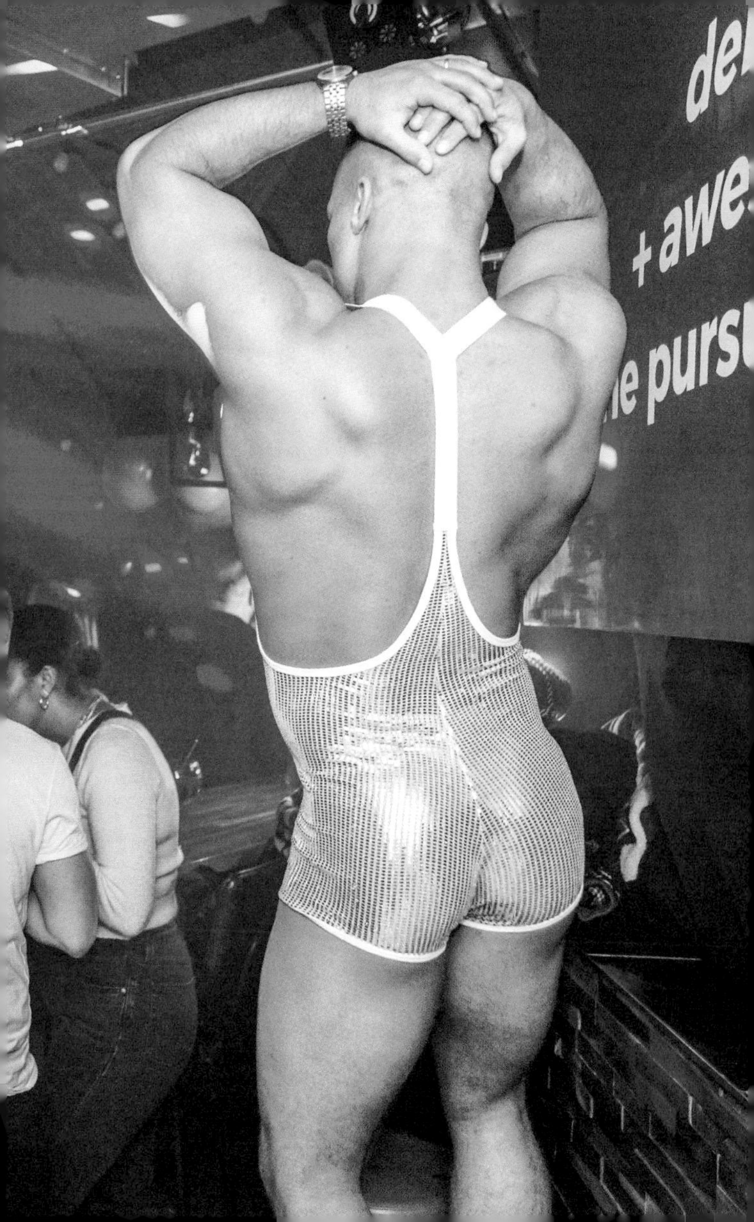

39

ROYAL
VAUXHALL TAVERN

Class act in queer performance

You can feel the history creaking out of every wooden corner, barely held up by the half dozen narrow cast-iron columns dotted around this iconic Grade II-listed venue. When it's packed to the gills (every Friday and Saturday night), the RVT feels like the centre of the universe, but it's best appreciated in its more intimate capacity as a theatre. Sunday Cabaret is a classic, but Bar Wotever, Not Another Drag Competition, and King of Clubs are all longstanding regular events that range from hilariously amateur to experimental and in-your-face. The secret's been out for a few decades though, so get your ticket in advance.

372 Kennington Lane, SE11 5HY
Nearest station: Vauxhall
vauxhalltavern.com @rvtofficial

40

THE TWO BREWERS

Vibrant performance powerhouse

With amateur talent shows, quizzes, weekly cabaret and karaoke nights, and Drag Race viewing
parties that capture all the fervour of a World Cup
final, this legendary bar draws a mixed crowd
seven nights a week and is the beating heart of
queer Clapham. The entertainment is more com-
fortably camp than cutting-edge, but the real
appeal is knowing you can drop by any week-
night and instantly feel at home. On weekends,
two dancefloors open up and transform the space
into a proper, heaving club, where you will likely
run into an ex, but no worries – as the night goes
on it becomes quite a meat market and you'll have
no trouble finding someone new to go home with.

114 Clapham High St, sw4 7UJ
Nearest station: Clapham Common
the2brewers.com @the2brewers

41

QUEERCIRCLE

Culture hub for all things queer

The proud anchor of Greenwich's new Design District, QUEERCIRCLE combines aspects of a community centre, bookshop and art gallery to really earn its 'culture hub' appellation. With three seasons per year, each featuring an exhibition by a contemporary queer artist in the main gallery, an archive exhibition in the library, and a residency in the project spaces upstairs, there's always a lot going on here. The 2,800 square-foot space simultaneously offers a peaceful refuge and a dynamic hive of like-minded art enthusiasts. It's as diverse as the queer community it serves – no mean feat – and well worth the trip.

3 Barton Yard, SE10 0BN
Nearest station: North Greenwich
queercircle.org @queercircle

42

THE VITO PROJECT

Haven for cinephiles in a former Victorian workhouse

The Cinema Museum hosts this monthly film club dedicated to pulling queer representation out of the celluloid closet. The screenings typically encompass the silent era and the golden age of Hollywood (you'll be amazed at some of the blatant homoerotica), and each is bookended by an erudite introduction and a panel discussion with energetic audience participation. When passionate opinions start flying around underneath the massive hammerbeam arches of this Grade II-listed former workhouse (where Charlie Chaplin spent time as a child), you'll understand the other, subtler mission of the Vito Project – to get young and old to bond over their love of film.

The Cinema Museum, 2 Dugard Way, SE11 4TH
Nearest stations: Kennington, Elephant & Castle
cinemamuseum.org.uk

43

LONDON LGBTQ+ COMMUNITY CENTRE

Sober sanctuary in Southwark

Your own living room to relax in right next to Tate Modern? Don't say being queer never got you anything! Simple, functional interiors belie the mammoth ambition behind this new intersectional safe space, where you can chill in a dedicated quiet room, grab a cheap cuppa at the cafe (£1 tea; £2 coffee), or join in a dazzling array of events and groups, from knitting workshops and foreign-language exchanges to yoga and meditation sessions, poetry circles, and mental-health support. It's a refreshing reminder that queers don't need booze to have a great time – we bring the party with us.

60–62 Hopton Street, SE1 9JH
Nearest station: Blackfriars
londonlgbtqcentre.org @ldnlgbtqcentre

44

OBERON

Heavenly haven with sublime cocktails

The 1930s decor – complete with authentic stained glass – sets the stage at this Art Nouveau and Midsummer Night's Dream-themed cocktail bar just off the Elephant roundabout. Proudly managed and operated by women, the gender balance is refreshing for a queer bar; it's broadly inclusive without being any particular scene – we're all just grateful to have a quality LGBTQ+ venue in the Elephant. The vibe is romantic (fantastic for date nights), creative (Sip & Paint art classes) and whimsical (regular gayming and comedy nights), and the weekend dance parties end up packed (free entry helps). Locals should make this a regular haunt, and we'll happily cross town again for another honey-raspberry margarita.

16, Draper House, SE1 6TH
Nearest station: Elephant & Castle
oberonbar.co.uk @oberonse1

45

THE WEEKENDING

Friendliest place to get pecs in the city

The routine is simple: Monday and Thursday are Push days (chest, shoulders, triceps); Tuesday and Friday are Pull days (back and biceps); and Wednesday and Saturday are legs and core. What's more complex is how Fabio Pozzetto managed to turn a pop-up outdoor workout session on Clapham Common into a welcoming community of fitness aficionados that somehow avoids the typical cliques that make so many other queer gyms insufferable. Granted, the clientele's chiselled physiques are intimidating at first (and skew heavily male, though all genders are welcome), but Fabio goes above and beyond to make his studio a safe and inclusive space. If you walk in ready to sweat, you're already part of the club.

Arch 6, Manor Place Depot, Angel Lane, SE17 3FR
Nearest station: Elephant & Castle
theweekending.co.uk @theweekending

46

56 DEAN STREET

Europe's largest MSM-focused sexual health clinic

Okay, we know, getting tested isn't anybody's idea of fun; that's exactly why the extraordinary team behind 56 Dean Street and Dean Street Express has made it as quick and painless as possible. The website makes booking a breeze, and the staff are unparalleled in their professionalism. Beyond routine testing with results in 24 hours, they also pioneered getting the NHS to cover PrEP, offer a specialist trans clinic every Wednesday called 56T, and host a variety of screening and counselling services. On your first visit, it's absolutely worth registering for a membership card, which makes your next appointment even easier.

56 and 34 Dean Street, WID 6AQ
Nearest station: Leicester Square
dean.st @56deanstreetofficial

47

ADMIRAL DUNCAN

Indomitable grande dame of Old Compton Street

Bombed in World War II before it was gay, and bombed again in 1999 *because* it was gay, the Admiral Duncan will endure long past its trendier neighbours. As the ground zero of gay Soho, it's an essential stop-off on any central London pub crawl, and the comfort of knowing it never really changes is part of the appeal. The solitary room will be bursting at the seams with every demographic, a queen 'of a certain age' will be belting out a show tune under the neon sign at the back, and you'll do a double take at how cheap your pint is, so stay for a few.

54 Old Compton Street, W1D 4UB
Nearest station: Leicester Square
admiral-duncan.co.uk @admiral_duncan

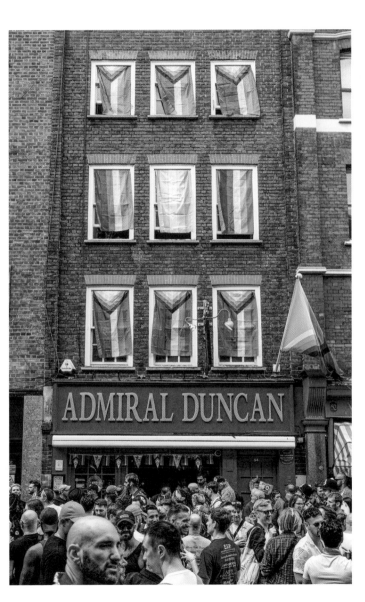

48

THE YARD BAR

Soho's best-known secret garden

When you're tired of being crammed into claustrophobic alcoves in tiny bars, make your way to The Yard – you'll still be squeezed in of course, but you can look up and see the night sky and get a breath of fresh air while still being fully immersed in the throbbing Soho scene (and here, the prices are worth the ambience). Your ears will stop ringing long enough to strike up a conversation, and if you grab a spot on the balcony upstairs you'll have the best people-watching spot in the West End. On lazy weekend afternoons, the leafy courtyard feels twice as big and downright continental, especially with an Aperol spritz and a cigarette.

57 Rupert Street, W1D 7PL
Nearest station: Piccadilly Circus
yardbar.co.uk @theyardsoho

49
BALANS SOHO NO. 60

Camp cuisine, with generous portions of both

When it comes to Old Compton Street's saturated food scene, Balans got there first (1987), and stays open the latest (6am). The menu is modern British and indulgent (the French toast has been described as 'life-changing'), but you come for the atmosphere, which gets cheekier and more outrageous as the night goes on. You'll see drag queens, but they're likely just downing a Bloody Mary before their shift down the street; here, the staff are the entertainment – bursting with banter and ready to give you the rundown on all the best places in Soho. It's not quite the celebrity haunt it once was (Gaga hasn't been seen here for over a decade), but the ambience and service make *you* feel like the superstar instead.

60-62 Old Compton Street, W1D 4UG
Nearest station: Leicester Square
balans.co.uk @balanslondon

50

THE FRIENDLY SOCIETY

Subterranean psychedelic speakeasy

No, you're not hallucinating – Barbie dolls really are swimming through floral bouquets superglued to the ceiling of this gaudy cocktail bar, the stools are garden gnomes, the back wall is plastered with alternating *Playgirl* and *Playboy* magazine covers, and a giant *Lesbian Jungle* book cover dominates the way to the toilet. If you've ever wondered what it's like to sip a perfectly decent £10.50 cocktail while sitting inside John Waters' brain, look no further. The bartenders live up to the name here, so don't be shy – they're proud of their quirky hole in the wall and happy to point out their favourite pieces of kitsch.

79 Wardour Street, W1D 6QG
Nearest stations: Piccadilly Circus, Leicester Square
@thefriendlysocietysoho

51

SOHO THEATRE

Comedy, theatre and everything in between

Queers are the gears that power all West End theatre, but Soho Theatre puts the LGBTQ+ experience centre stage, regularly showcasing the vanguard of queer talent, from cabaret and drag kings to coming-of-age comedies like Amrou Al-Kadhi's *Glamrou: from Qur'an to Queen*. With six shows a day across three different stages, you're spoilt for choice, but the Cabaret & Drag Labs offer something unique: a ten-week workshop where curious amateurs develop their own act under the mentorship of some of London's leading performers. It's supportive, inclusive, practical (you're taught how to self-promote as well as sashay) and a vivid illustration of Soho Theatre's connection to the community.

21 Dean Street, W1D 3NE
Nearest station: Tottenham Court Road
sohotheatre.com @sohotheatre

52

REGULATION

Soho's kinkiest shop

Get a birthday card at Prowler, maybe some cute cut-offs at Clonezone, then turn the corner to experience a real sex shop. Regulation is unadulterated fetish: portable power packs for electro chastity belts; slings and suspension frames; premium full-body leather outfits; and a £650 Fuck Machine proudly on display downstairs. Don't be intimidated – they have all your vanilla kink accessories as well as the hardcore, but better curated and presented in an uncluttered space that feels more gallery than gift shop. Citizens of other cities have to buy this stuff discreetly online; Londoners can check it out on their lunch breaks.

13A Bateman Street, W1D 3AF
Nearest station: Tottenham Court Road
regulation.co.uk @regulationstore

53

SHE SOHO

London's last lesbian bar

Every London lesbian knows She, the focal point of the city's lesbian nightlife, and that familiarity brings with it a home-away-from-home vibe that's rare in central London. Everyone knows everyone – but even if you don't, with a capacity of only 80, it's only a matter of time before you're chatting up the new girl in the corner. She Soho keeps it interesting throughout the week with karaoke, quiz nights, burlesque, and drag king competitions, and weekends are rowdy dance parties with a queue down the street.

23a Old Compton Street, W1D 5JL
Nearest station: Leicester Square
@shesohobar

54

TATE BRITAIN LGBTQIA+ TOUR

A journey through queer art history

From the surprisingly direct *Sappho and Erinna* to the enigmatic *Cholmondeley Ladies*, queer art is everywhere in the Tate's collections but all too often you wouldn't know it from just reading the exhibition labels. These free tours, usually every Saturday from 3pm, aim to rectify that. There's a certain thrill in discovering some of these queer histories as described in artworks from the 17th century to the present day, but the real highlights are the conversations facilitated by the erudite guides. Voice your own thoughts about what Marlow Moss' geometry says about the trans experience, or Hockney's paintings reveal about being a gay man in the 1970s – you share something with these artists and your interpretation is valid.

Millbank, SW1P 4RG
Nearest station: Pimlico
tate.org.uk @tate

55

V & A LGBTQIA+ TOURS

Treasure chest of queer artefacts

Three simple criteria – the object must be made by a queer person, depict a queer person, or have been adopted by the queer community as something meaningful – have been applied to open up the vast V&A collection to a secret history that the passionate museum guides can't wait to share. A portrait miniature of James I gives a clue as to why it was quipped that 'Elizabeth was King; now James is Queen.' Rodin's *Metamorphosis of Ovid* tells a classical trans love story with a happy ending. You'll even learn about the pivotal role that former V&A curator Carl Winter played in decriminalising homosexuality in the UK. Guided tours take place on the last Saturday of the month, but you can download your own 'Out on Display' guide to the collections.

Cromwell Road, SW7 2RL
Nearest station: South Kensington
vam.co.uk @vamuseum

IMAGE CREDITS

Intro pp.2–9, ©Aneta Pruszynska feat. Charlie Hopkins; ©Harry Elletson courtesy Clapham Grand; ©Captured by Corinne; Holly Whitaker; Maartje Hensen @maartjehensen; Róisín Murphy; By entry number: 1, Vera Jacquet; 2, Steve Gregson/London Gay Men's Chorus; 3, ©Maartje Hensen @maartjehensen; 4, ©Linda Brindley; 5, Kathleen Arundell Photography, Bishopsgate Institute; 6, First image Bailey-Cooper Photography/Alamy Stock Photo; second image ©Harvey Williams-Fairley courtesy House of Trash; third image ©Kiev Rø courtesy House of Trash; 7, First image David Pearson/Alamy Stock Photo; second image Gregory Wrona/Alamy Stock Photo; third image A.P.S. (UK)/Alamy Stock Photo; 8, First & second images ©Rahil Ahmad; third image ©John Sturrock, both courtesy Queer Britain; 9, Atlas Grinds; 10, Queer Garden feat. Olly Alexander; 11, Chloe Rice Writer & Natasha Roland; 12, Sydney McCourt, Opening Doors' Silver Pride Tea Dance 2022; 13, First image ©Gulja Holland; second image ©Charlotte West-Williams for Disco 54; 14, ©Ivie Bartlett; 15, ©Victor Hensel-Coe; 16, ©Phoenix Edwards, phoenixtakesphotos.co.uk; 17, Dom Martin for Colour Factory; 18, ©Rebecca Zephyr Thomas; 19, All images ©Captured by Corinne; 20, First image ©Luke Dyson; second image ©Gemma Bell; 21, Róisín Murphy feat. (l-r) Lucinda B. Hind, Soroya Marchelle, Mahatma Khandi & PMBC; 22, First & second images ©Glodi Miessi; third image ©Captured by Corinne; 23, Courtesy Guts Gallery and Eva Herzog Photography; 24, ©Milan Bures for The New York Times; 25, ©Maartje Hensen @ maartjehensen; 26, Prudence Cuming courtesy The Gilbert & George Centre; 27, First image Andy Matthews-VIEW/Alamy Stock Photo; second image Dan Govan, lightbydan.com; 28, Wanda Martin; 29, ©Aneta Pruszynska; 30, ©Luke Dyson, Mighty Hoopla 2022; 31, Zefrog/ Alamy Stock Photo; 32, BFI/Millie Turner; 33, ©Michael T Smith courtesy Philip Normal; 34, First image Jan Klos; second image Chris Martchant; third image Rebecca Zephyr Thomas; 35, Simon Balson/Alamy Stock Photo; 36, ©Captured by Corinne; 37, ©Henri T @ documentedbyhenrit; 38, ©Nicolas Chinardet, zefrographica; 39, Pat Tuson/Alamy Stock Photo; 40, Photo ©ChrisJepson.com; 41, First image QUEERCIRCLE ©Taran Wilkhu; second image installation view from The Queens' Jubilee!, at QUEERCIRCLE ©Deniz Guzel; 42, John Gaffen/Alamy Stock Photo; 43, Tim Boddy; 44, ©Antic Pubs; 45, Alex Charovas; 46, David Cliff/SOPA Images/LightRocket via Getty Images; 47, Stephen Chung/ Alamy Live News; 48, Tony Farrugia/Alamy Stock Photo; 49, First image Joe Howard; second image Fotomatador/Alamy Stock Photo; 50, First image Antonello Sticca; second image ATGlamourLondon, model Donna Wildcard, makeup by HollyArtistry; 51, Jonathan Birch for Soho Theatre; 52, Regulation; 53, ©Phoenix Edwards, phoenixtakesphotos.co.uk; 54, Malcolm Park editorial/Alamy Live News; 55, www.alanwilliamsphotography.com

CONTRIBUTORS

Like so many Londoners, *Frank Gallaugher* is an immigrant – from New Orleans, in his case. Calling the capital home for over a decade now, he edits art books by day, learns French by night, and spends his weekends cruising the canals (not like that – on his narrowboat, with his boyfriend and cat).

Hoxton Mini Press is a small indie publisher based in east London. We make books about London (and beyond) with a dedication to lovely, sustainable production and brilliant photography. When we started the company, people told us 'print was dead'; we wanted to prove them wrong. Books are no longer about information but objects in their own right: things to collect and own and inspire. We are an environmentally conscious publisher, committed to offsetting our carbon footprint. This book, for instance, is 100 per cent carbon compensated, with offset purchased from Stand for Trees.

INDEX

An Opinionated Guide to Queer London
First edition

Published in 2023 by Hoxton Mini Press, London
Copyright © Hoxton Mini Press 2023. All rights reserved.

Text by Frank Gallaugher
Copy-editing by Gaynor Sermon
Design by Richard Mason
Production by Sarah-Louise Deazley
Proofreading by Octavia Stocker
Production and editorial support by Georgia Williams

With thanks to Matthew Young for initial series design.

Please note: we recommend checking the websites listed for each
entry before you visit for the latest information on price, opening times
and pre-booking requirements.

The right of Frank Gallaugher to be identified as the creator of this Work has
been asserted under the Copyright, Designs and Patents Act 1988.

No part of this publication may be reproduced, stored in a retrieval system,
or transmitted in any form or by any means, electronic, mechanical,
photocopying, recording or otherwise, without the prior written permission
of the copyright owner.

A CIP catalogue record for this book is available from the British Library.

ISBN: 978-1-914314-47-6

Printed and bound by OZGraf, Poland

Hoxton Mini Press is an environmentally conscious publisher, committed
to offsetting our carbon footprint. This book is 100 percent carbon
compensated, with offset purchased from Stand For Trees.

For every book you buy from our website, we plant a tree:
www.hoxtonminipress.com

MIX
Paper from
responsible sources
FSC
www.fsc.org
FSC® C163799